LITTLE STORIES ABOUT GOD

Faith, Hope and Charity

With Faith we know God.

With Hope we trust that if we are good, God will give us a great reward in Heaven.

With Charity we love God and our neighbor.

Little Stories about GOD

by

Mary Reynolds McDonald

Illustrated by

The Daughters of St. Paul

ST. PAUL EDITIONS

IMPRIMATUR:

✠ Daniel J. Gercke

Episcopus Tucsonensis

Library of Congress Catalog Card Number: 64-22430

ISBN 0-8198-0080-5 (cloth)
ISBN 0-8198-0081-3 (paper)

Printed in the U.S.A. by the Daughters of St. Paul
50 St. Paul's Ave., Jamaica Plain, Boston, MA 02130

In thanksgiving for the

miraculous recovery

of my little boy

from a very serious illness,

I gratefully dedicate

this little book

to

St. Euphrasia Pelletier

MARY   REYNOLDS   MCDONALD

INTRODUCTION

How these "Little Stories about God" came to be.

When my children were very little—too young for school—we lived in a remote, desolate, desert area of the great South West.

We had church services only once a month. On other Sundays we lighted our candles and knelt to say our little prayers.

Having been a teacher before my marriage, I decided to teach my children about God in my own little way.

The first story I told was on and about "Easter". I put all I had of devotion and dramatics into the telling, and my little daughter was so thrilled that she repeated it over and over to her dolls!

I was amazed that she remembered it so well, and her reaction made a deep impression upon me. I began at once to develop the idea about God and His loving closeness to us.

When, at last, the Stories were finished, I was in a quandry about what to call them. I discussed it with the children, and my little boy, then about six, said, "Mother, I like all the stories you've told us, but I think I like best the "Little Stories about God."

MARY REYNOLDS MCDONALD

Contents

God Is Our Father

My child, it is growing dark,
Soon it will be time for sleep.
You have been a good child today.
Mother loves you and God loves you.
God is glad when you are good.

15

I must tell you about God.
He is our Father in Heaven.
He watches over us all day and all night.
He is kind and loving.
He wants us to love Him.
He wants us to be good children.
Then some day we shall go
    to see Him in Heaven.
Tonight you are very tired.
You have been playing all day.
God has been with you.
He has taken care of you.
He will always love you.
Let us say,
Thank You, dear God,
    for taking care of me today.
I want to know You better.
I want to love You.

The Sign of the Cross

It is morning dear.
    Another day has come.
Last night we thanked God
    for taking care of us all day.

Now we must say **Thank You** again.
We must thank Him for His care all through the
    night.
It is easy to talk to God.
    People call it praying.
When we pray we make the sign of the Cross.
When we are afraid of anything
    we make the sign of the Cross.

17

When we go to sleep at night we make the sign of
   the Cross.
When we open our eyes in the morning we make the
   sign of the Cross.
Give me your right hand, dear.
I will help you make the sign of the Cross.
I will help you say the words:

In the name of the Father,

and of the Son,

and of the Holy Spirit. Amen.

Three Persons in One God

There are many things to learn about God.
No one on earth knows all about Him.
As long as you live you will find out new things about
   Him.
Every day you will learn more about Him.
Every day you will love Him more.

There is one thing about Him that is very strange.
It cannot be understood by any one.
It is this: There are three Persons in God.
They are the Father, the Son, and the Holy Spirit.

The Father is God.

The Son is God.

The Holy Spirit is God.

Yet there is only one God.

Now let us learn this little prayer:

**Glory be to the Father,
and to the Son,
and to the Holy Spirit,
as it was in the beginning,
is now and ever shall be,
world without end.
Amen.**

In the picture you can see an Angel.

God made the Angels.

He made them beautiful.

God and the Angels live in a place called Heaven.

Some of the Angels grew tired of being good.

They did not mind God.

God had to send them away.

So He made a place for them. It is a place of
    ugliness called Hell.

These bad angels are called devils. They do not want
    us to mind God.

They want us to sin so that we shall not go to
    Heaven.

Now, God loves us very much.

He wants us to be good. He wants us to go to
    Heaven.

24

He has given each one of us a good Angel.
This good Angel guards us day and night.
We should love our Guardian Angel. We should
talk to him often.

Let us learn this little prayer:

Angel of God

**Angel of God,
my guardian dear,
To whom God's love entrusts me here,
Ever this day be at my side
to watch and guard,
to rule and guide.**

26

The World

God is our Father in Heaven.
He has always lived and He always will live.
God made the world. He made the animals.

He made the birds.
He made the fishes and the creeping things.

He made the trees and the flowers.
He made the sun and the moon and the stars.
He made the rivers and the seas and the lakes.

They were very beautiful. He made them out of
  nothing.
Only God could do that. Isn't that wonderful, my
  child?
God made all those beautiful things out of nothing.
Let us think about it.
Let us say, **Thank You, God,**
For making this big, beautiful world.

Man

After God made the world and all the other
    beautiful things
He said, **Let us make man.**
Then He did a very wonderful thing.
He took some earth and shaped it like a man.
Then He gave him a soul.
God called the man Adam.
He made Adam not quite so beautiful as the Angels.

God made him master over all earthly things.
He was above all other things because he had a soul.
The soul lives forever.
Animals do not have souls that will live forever.
They do not know about God.

Woman

God loved Adam.
He wanted him to be happy.
God thought it was not good for Adam to be alone.
He wanted to give him a helper.
Then He put Adam to sleep.
He took a rib from Adam's side.
Out of it He made a woman.
God called her Eve.
He brought her to Adam.

33

Adam was glad to have Eve for his helper.
Adam and Eve were our first parents.
God made them with His own hands.
They were very good and happy.

The Garden

Adam and Eve lived in the garden of Eden.

It was a very beautiful garden.

God told them where to find food.

Then He pointed to one tree.
Do not eat the fruit of that tree, He said.
For a while Adam and Eve were good.
They were very, very happy.
Flowers bloomed at their feet.
Birds sang in the trees.

God came and talked to them often.
They loved to talk to God.
He was so kind to them.
He was their loving Father.
He is our loving Father, too.

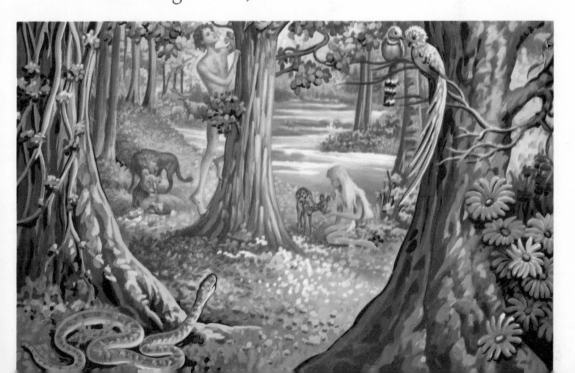

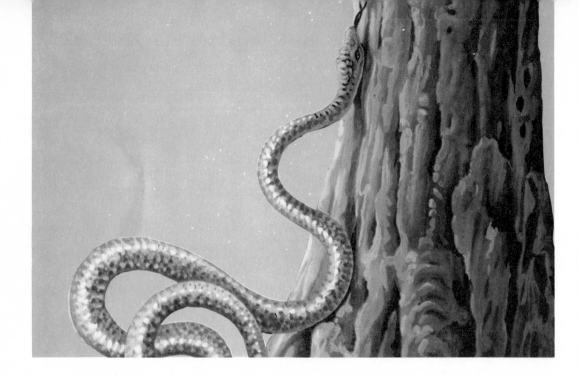

The First Mistake

The devil saw Adam and Eve in the garden.
He did not like to see them so happy.
One day he changed himself into a snake.

He went to Eve and said, **Why do you not eat the fruit of that tree?**

God told us not to, she said.

Then the devil laughed at her.

The devil hates God. He tries to make everyone disobey Him.

Eve did not like to be laughed at.

The devil said to her, **Go and eat the fruit of that tree.**

It will make you very smart.

Poor Eve!

I wish she had not listened to the devil.

I wish she had said, **Go away, you ugly thing!**

But Eve made a big mistake.

She did not send the devil away.

She listened to him.

She went over to the tree.

She took the fruit in her hand.

40

She tasted it.
Then she gave it to Adam.
He tasted it too. Poor Adam!

The Fear of God

Very soon Adam and Eve heard God's voice.
On other days they had run to meet Him.
But now they were afraid.
They knew they had sinned.
They knew that God was angry.
They hid behind bushes.
That was a silly thing to do.
No one can hide from God.
He sees everything we do.

He said to Adam, **Why did you disobey Me?**
Adam said, **Eve gave me the fruit and I ate it.**
Then God said to them,
You must leave this lovely garden.
You have sinned.

You and your children must suffer for it.
You must work hard.
Sorrow and pain will come to you.
Death will come to you.

God's Promise

God drove Adam and Eve from the garden.
Then He closed the gate.
He placed an Angel before the gate.
The Angel held a flaming sword in his hand.
Adam and Eve could not go back.
How sad they were!
Their sin had caused all the sorrow that would come
    to God's beautiful world.

I think Eve cried.
God still loved Adam and Eve.
They were His children.
He felt sorry for them.

Some day, He said, another woman will come.

She will obey Me.

She will crush the ugly head of the snake.

She will bring joy to the world.

She will be the mother of the Savior.
The Savior will be My Son.
He will suffer very, very much.
He will atone for the sins of the world.
He will open the gates of Heaven.

Cain and Abel

After a while Adam and Eve had two sons.
Their names were Cain and Abel.
One day they had a fight.
Cain killed his brother Abel.

48

What a big sin that was!

God punished Cain.

He sent him away from his home.

Adam and Eve were sad.

Eve said to Adam, **God told us we should suffer for
  our sins.**

They knew that because they had disobeyed God
  it was hard for their children to be good.

All of us are born with the sin of Adam on our souls.

It is called "original" sin.

It is taken away when we are baptized.

49

Noe

After a time Adam and Eve had another son.
They named him Seth.
He was a good man and his children were good.
Cain, his brother, was always bad.
His children were bad, too.
By and by the world was full of bad people.
There was one man who was good and God loved
    him.

He was of the family of Seth. His name was Noe.
God told Noe to build a big ship (ark) and go into it.
Noe took his three sons and their wives with him.
He took two of each of the animals and birds and
    beasts.

Then God sent a rain storm.
It lasted for forty days and forty nights.
It rained so much that all the people were drowned.
All the animals were drowned, too.
Only the people and the animals and the birds on
    the ark were saved.

God sent the storm because the people were so bad.
They did not love God. They did not pray to Him.
They did not mind Him.

The Tower of Babel

When the storm was over, Noe thanked God.
Soon the land was dry.
Then he and his children came out of the ship.
All the animals and birds and beasts came, too.
After many years the world was full of people again.
For a while they were good.
By and by they began to get bad.
They had learned to do many wonderful things.

They thought they were very smart.
They became very proud.
We will build a tower that will be as high as heaven,
    they said.
They started to build it.
God punished them in a new way.
He made them talk strangely.
They could not tell what their friends were saying.
They could not help one another.
They were just like strangers then.
They stopped working on the Tower of Babel.
They went to faraway lands.

Moses

Noe had three sons.
Their names were Sem, Ham and Japheth.
From Sem's family came a man named Abraham.
He was a good man.
God told him that from his family the Savior would
    come.
Many of the people forgot about God.
They grew tired of praying for the Savior to come.
They made images and worshipped them.
That made the good people sad.
At that time there lived a man named Moses.

52

Moses was a good man.

He was a leader of men.

One day God gave him two large slates of stone.

Upon them were written the ten commandments.

They were ten rules for being good.

Moses taught them to the people.

Some day you will learn them.

God wants you to know them and to keep them.

One of them says that we must obey father and
mother.

God has promised great blessings to children that
obey.

The Angel Gabriel

Many, many years went by.

The time for the Savior came.

God chose Mary to be the mother of the Savior.

Mary was pure and holy.

She had never, never sinned.

She was the wife of St. Joseph.

One day, as she was praying, a bright light shone
     about her.

She saw the Angel Gabriel.

Hail (Mary) **full of grace, the Lord is with thee;**
Blessed art thou among women, he said.
Mary was very humble. She was afraid.
Then the Angel said, **Don't be afraid, Mary.**
God wants you to be the mother of His Son.
Mary said, **I will obey God.**
I will be His handmaid.
I will do as He says.
Then the Angel Gabriel smiled and went back to
　　Heaven.

Mary's Visit

Mary's heart was full of joy.
Mary said, **I will go to see my Cousin Elizabeth.**
I will give her some of my happiness.
When Elizabeth opened her door and saw Mary
　　standing there, a strange thing happened.
Elizabeth said to Mary, **Blessed art thou among**
　　women and blessed is the fruit of thy womb.
The Holy Ghost had told Elizabeth about the Holy
　　Child that was coming to Mary.
Wasn't that wonderful?
Mary was so happy that she began to sing.
She sang a beautiful song.

It has some big words in it but some day you will
    learn it.

All the people shall call me blessed.

That is part of her song.

It is true. Every day we call her blessed.

Every day we say the prayer she loves.

    **Hail Mary, full of grace, the Lord is with thee;
Blessed art thou among women and blessed is
the fruit of thy womb, Jesus. Holy Mary, Mother
of God, pray for us sinners now and at the hour
of our death. Amen.**

John

Mary stayed with Elizabeth for a long time.
She helped Elizabeth with her work.
She was kind and sweet to her.
Soon St. Elizabeth's baby came.
He was named John.
When he was a man he baptized Jesus.
That's why we call him St. John the Baptist.
About the time that St. Elizabeth's baby came, Mary
went to her home in Nazareth.
She had to get ready for the Baby that was coming
to her.
In those days mothers could not go to the shops and
buy cloth.
They had to make it at home.
Mary had to spin flax into threads.
Then she had to weave it into wide bands to wrap
around her baby.
She had to weave soft, little, woolly blankets to keep
Him warm, too.
How Mary must have loved getting ready for Jesus!
Some day Jesus will come to you.
You must get ready for Him now.
Ask Holy Mary, Mother of God, to help you.

Bethlehem

The days passed quickly.
Soon Mary had finished all the baby clothes.
Soon the Baby Jesus would come.
How Mary longed for Him to come!
Your mother longed for you to come, too.
Most mothers try to be like the mother of Jesus.
That's why we love our mothers so much.
That's why we obey them always.
Well, about that time the ruler of the land sent a
    letter to all the people.
It said that everyone should go to their chief city.
Everyone should write his name in a big book.
It was a long way to Bethlehem.
Mary was very tired but she obeyed the law.
We must go at once, she said to St. Joseph.
Mary made a little bundle of the baby clothes.
She gave it to St. Joseph to carry for her.
She closed all the windows of her little house.
Then she closed the door.
They walked and walked and walked.
Poor, sweet, tired, little mother, I love you so!
You were always doing the will of God.
You did not think of yourself at all.
You were like an Angel—so beautiful and good.

The First Christmas

By and by Mary and Joseph came to Bethlehem.

Mary was very tired after her long trip.

St. Joseph told her to sit down and rest.

He went from house to house asking for a place
for her to stay.

No, we have no room, said each one of them.

Then St. Joseph went to the inn.

He wished so much that Mary could have a good,
clean bed in which to rest.

No, we have no room, said the innkeeper.

How sadly St. Joseph must have told Mary that!

They walked slowly back to the hills.

At last they found a cave in the side of a hill.

There in the cave Mary lay down to sleep.

She was humble and poor.

I think she said, **Thank You, God, for my straw bed.**

I am so tired tonight.

About midnight Mary heard Angels singing.

A beautiful light shone about her.

There beside her was a little Baby Boy.
It was Jesus, the Savior.
That was the first Christmas.

The Birthday Song

At that time shepherds were watching their flocks
of sheep on the hillside.
All at once they heard sweet music. They looked
up and saw Angels.
The Angels were singing a beautiful song.

60

Glory to God in the highest, and on earth peace to
men of good will, they sang.
The shepherds were poor, humble men.
They had not gone to school. They did not know
many things.
They were like little children.
When they saw the Angels they were afraid.
Don't be afraid, the biggest Angel said. We bring
you good, glad news.
Joy has come to the world. Today the Savior is born.
You will find Him lying in a manger.
The shepherds looked at one another.
Can this be the Promised One? they said. Let us
go and see.

The Shepherds

The Angels went singing back to Heaven.
The shepherds got up from their knees.
In the distance they saw a beautiful light.
They followed it and found a cave in the hillside.
It was a stable where animals came at night to
sleep.

61

There in the manger lay the Savior.
He was wrapped in the white linen bands that Mary
    had made with her own, sweet hands.
Mary and Joseph were kneeling beside the manger.
A light from Heaven filled the stable.
The animals gazed in wide-eyed wonder.
Their big, warm bodies helped to heat the cave.
They warmed the Baby Jesus with their breath.
The shepherds knelt at the feet of Jesus.
They adored the new-born King.
They gave Him their little soft, white woolly lambs.

Because He wished to be like other babies, Jesus
did not speak to them.
If He had, I think He would have said, **The gift I
want is you.**
Child, give Me your heart.
Let us play that we are the shepherds.
Each time that we go into the church let us go
quietly to the altar.
Let us give ourselves to Jesus.
Let us say to Him, **Little Jesus, I am all Yours.**
Keep me always near You.

Jesus

The shepherds went back to their flocks. They were
filled with joy.
They told everyone they met the good, glad news.
Christ, the Savior, the Promised One, has come, they
said.
Everybody was glad.
On the eighth day St. Joseph gave the Child a name.
He named Him "Jesus."
That is the name He had been called by the Angel.

63

Whenever we hear the Holy Name of Jesus we bow
our heads.

It is the very sweetest of all names.

Jesus' birthday and the day on which He was named
are Holydays.

Everyone goes to church on those days.

They are happy days of prayer and joy and feasting.

The Holy Child Jesus with His great love brings joy
to the world each Christmas.

He brings peace to people of good will.

To be of good will means to be kind.

Let us think kind thoughts. Let us say kind words.

Let us do kind deeds. Then we shall have peace.

The Rich Kings

In a far away land in the East there lived three
wise men.

They were rich kings.

They knew a great deal about the holy books.

The books told them that it was about time for the
Savior to be born.

One night they saw a beautiful star in the sky.

It was not like other stars. It was very bright and
beautiful.

64

It seemed to hang low in the sky. It seemed to speak
  to them.

They said, **Let us take our best gifts. Let us follow
  the star.**

It will lead us to the Promised One.

They set out riding upon camels. They traveled for
  a long time.

At last they came to Jerusalem. They went to King
  Herod.

They asked him where they would find the new
  born King of the Jews.

65

Herod did not know. **When you find Him, come and tell me.**

I want to see Him, too, said Herod.

At last the Magi (that's another name for the wise men) saw the star shining over a stable.

How glad they were to find Jesus!

They went in and knelt at His Feet.

They saw Mary, His Mother.

They saw Joseph, her kind husband.

They gave their rich gifts to the Baby Jesus.

Their gifts were gold, incense and myrrh.

The Baby Jesus in the Church

Mary and Joseph knew all the laws of the church.

They obeyed them, every one.

There was a law given to the people by Moses.

It was that babies should be brought to the church.

They should be given to God.

Mary obeyed that law though she did not have to.

Her Baby was God.

When parents gave their babies to God they brought a gift to the church.

Rich parents brought rich gifts.

Mary and Joseph were poor.

They brought the gifts of the poor—a pair of doves.

66

While they were in the church a holy priest came in.
His name was Simeon.
God had told him that he should not die until he
    had seen the Savior.
Simeon raised his eyes toward Heaven.
He sang a song.
Some day you must learn it.
**Now, O Lord, let me die in peace, for my eyes have
    seen the Savior.**
That is part of his song.
Then he turned to Mary, the sweet Mother of Jesus.
O Mother, he said, **a sword of sorrow will pierce
    your heart.**
I think tears came to his eyes when he told Mary
    that.

Jesus Christ—The King

The three kings were rich and wise.
Best of all, they were good.
Their souls were filled with humility.
God blessed them.
He led them to the feet of Jesus.
God loves all people—rich and poor.
He sent singing Angels to tell the poor shepherds
    of Jesus' birth.

He sent a beautiful star to guide the rich kings to
    Baby Jesus.
He wants us to know that we all belong to Him.
God is our Father.
He is Christ, the King.
We are His children, the children of a King.
So we are princes and princesses.
We must always remember that.
We must be noble and good.
We must play fair.
We must show that we belong to Christ, the King.
We must be polite and kind to everyone.
Then our goodness will be like a light shining.
It will guide others to Jesus Christ, the Savior.

St. Joseph's Dream

After the Magi had adored Jesus they went away.
While they were sleeping an Angel came to them.
He said, **Do not tell Herod where the Christ Child is.**
Go home by another way.
They did as the Angel told them.
It so happened that while Joseph was sleeping an Angel came to him.
He said, **Joseph, arise; take the Child and His mother and go into Egypt.**
Herod wants to kill Baby Jesus.
Stay there until I tell you to leave.
Poor St. Joseph! How he hated to tell Mary that sad news.
He went over to the place where Mary slept.
In her arms the Baby Jesus lay sleeping.
St. Joseph laid his hand upon her.
Mary, Mary, he said,
An Angel has told me to take you and the Baby and go into Egypt.
Herod, the wicked king, is looking for Him.
He will kill Jesus.
Mary got up at once.
She wrapped her Holy Child in a woolly blanket.
Joseph helped her mount the little donkey.

Mary held the Baby Jesus close to her heart.
Long before day came they were far away.

Herod

Herod was a very bad man. He was not fit to be
    king.
He loved riches and power too much.
He loved himself more than God.
Because he was so bad he was not happy.
He was always afraid of losing his kingdom.
The Magi had told him of the new-born King of
    the Jews.
That worried him.
The Magi had not gone back to tell him where they
    had found the new-born King.
That made him angry.
Then he did a most cruel thing.
He made his soldiers go all over his kingdom.
They killed all the little boy babies of two years
    and under.
He thought that, in that way, he would kill Christ,
    the King.
But God takes care of His own.
The Baby, His mother and good St. Joseph were
    far away.
And they were safe.

70

Nazareth

Jesus and Mary and Joseph were happy in Egypt.
Mary took care of the Holy Child.
Her heart was always full of joy. They were in Egypt
    for a long time.
It did not seem long because they were so happy.
By and by the time came for them to leave.
An Angel came to St. Joseph in a dream.
Herod is dead, he said. **Now you may go back to
    Nazareth.**
How glad they were to go! They loved their little
    home.
It was a Holy Shrine. All homes should be like it.
Fathers should copy St. Joseph.
Mothers should copy Mary.
Children should copy the Child Jesus.
Then all the world would be full of happy homes.
Let us do all we can to make our homes happy.
Let us be quick to mind our parents.
Then God will bless us.

Jesus' Childhood

Jesus, Mary and Joseph are loved as the Holy
    Family.
They lived very quietly in Nazareth.

They did not tell anyone that Jesus was
    the Son of God.
The Holy Bible does not tell us much about those
    happy years.
It says only that the Boy Jesus grew strong and wise.
There is only one story told about Jesus' boyhood.
It is the story about Jesus in the church.
It is a very sad story because Jesus' mother
    must have felt the sword of sorrow
    pierce her heart.

72

She must have thought of what the holy Simeon
    had told her that day when she brought
    the Holy Child to the church for the first time.
Poor Joseph was sad, too.
There is a lesson for us in the story
    of the little lost Jesus.
Let us think about it.

The Boy Jesus in the Temple

It was in the Spring time. All the people were in
    Jerusalem.
(That's where the big church was.)
There was just one church where they went to
    worship and to offer sacrifices.
On the holydays that were kept by the Jews, all
    the people came to the Holy City to fast and
    pray.
Mary and Joseph were there, and also Jesus.
He was now twelve years old. For seven days this
    solemn feast lasted.
By and by the time came to go home. Mary walked
    with the women.
Joseph walked with the men.
Each thought that Jesus was with the other.
When night came they stopped to rest.

It was then they learned that Jesus was not there.
Poor Mary! It was the first time she had ever been
without Him.
What sorrow she felt!
Joseph, she said, **we must go back to Jerusalem.**
I cannot rest until we find Him.
They went back to the city.
For three days they looked for Him.
At last they found Him in the church, talking to the
priests.
Jesus, said Mary, **why have You done this?**
**Your father (St. Joseph) and I have been looking
everywhere for you.**
We were worried and sad.
Jesus said, **Mother, do you not know that I must
be about My Father's (God's) business?**

Sorrow

Sin is very ugly.
It stains our souls.
We lose Jesus when we sin.
Mary, the mother of Jesus, never sinned.
No sin ever soiled her pure white soul.
Yet she knows the sorrow of losing Jesus.

74

I think God let her suffer that pain
so that she would know how sad it is for us
when we lose Jesus.
Mary does not want us to lose Jesus.
But if we should ever lose Him,
we must go to Mary quickly.
She will know how sad we are.
She will help us to find our way back to Jesus.
Let us say often with all our hearts:
Holy Mary, Mother of God, pray for us sinners.
Now and at the hour of our death. Amen.

Jesus was twelve years old when Mary lost Him in the Holy City.

We do not hear about Jesus again until He became a big Man.

He was thirty years old.

The time had come for Him to begin His work as Savior of the world.

About that time a holy man came out of the desert.

He told everyone to be sorry for their sins.

He told them that the Savior was near.

Soon He will come to speak to you.

Get ready to meet Him, he said.

Great crowds came to hear this holy man.

He baptized them in the River Jordan.

His name was John. He was called "The Baptist."

One day Jesus walked down to the river.

He went to St. John to be baptized. St. John was very humble.

He said, **You are the Son of God. I should be baptized by You.**

But Jesus was very humble, too.

He was the great God, yet He was the most humble of all men.

76

He asked St. John to baptize Him.

St. John did as He wished.

Then the heavens opened.

A dove rested on Jesus' Head.

A voice from Heaven said, **This is My dear Son.**

Listen to Him.

Do as He tells you.

Forty Days

After Jesus was baptized He went into the desert.
There He stayed for forty days.

For forty days He did not eat.

He prayed to God the Father.

In Lent we copy Jesus' time in the desert.

We fast and pray.

We draw near to God.

At the end of Jesus' forty days of fasting and
prayer He was hungry.

The devil tried to make Jesus sin.

But Jesus told the devil to go away.

He could not make Jesus sin.

Then the devil left Him.

Angels came and gave Him food.

Jesus did that to show us how to be good.

The devil tries to make us sin, too.

We must not listen to the devil.
We must say, **Go away!**

I will not sin.
I love Jesus too much.

Peace and joy will come to us then.

Jesus, the Lamb of God

The time of fasting and prayer was over.
Jesus walked down to the River Jordan.
When John the Baptist saw Him he said,
Behold, the Lamb of God!
Behold Him who will take away the sins of the
world.
The people looked at one another.
They did not know what St. John meant.
The next day Jesus went again to the river.
St. John the Baptist saw Him.
There is the Lamb of God, he said.
Two young men looked at Jesus.
Then they came near to Him.
Jesus looked at them sweetly.
He said, **What do you wish?**

They said to Him, **Master, where do You live?**
Jesus said, **Come and see.**
They followed Him to a little shack by the river.
He talked to them about Heaven.
They felt sure that He was the Promised One.
They were John and Andrew.
They were the first of the twelve Apostles.

The Apostles

Andrew and John were thrilled.
They had sat in Jesus' little house.
They had listened to Him talk all the afternoon.
That evening Andrew told his brother Simon that
    he had found the Savior.
The next day Simon went with Andrew to Jesus.
Jesus was glad to meet Simon.
Jesus said to Him,
Your name is Simon.
You are the son of Jona.
I am going to change your name to Peter.
Now, my child, Peter means ROCK.
Jesus had big plans for Peter.
He was going to give him a great place in His
    Church.

80

Jesus came upon earth to teach us how to save
our souls.

Jesus knew that in a few years He would go back
to Heaven.

He had to leave teachers on earth to do His work.

So Jesus chose twelve men.

They were called Apostles.

They followed Him everywhere.

He taught them many things.

He gave them many graces.

They became good and holy because they loved
Jesus.

Follow Me

Jesus did not choose all the Apostles at one time.

People came out to hear Him talk.

He went about from place to place.

He chose the Apostles from the people who came
to hear Him.

The first two were John and Andrew.

Then came Peter, the fisherman.

Soon after that Jesus saw Philip.

81

He was a fisherman, too.

Jesus said to him, **Follow Me.**

Philip was glad to follow Jesus.

Philip told his friend to come and see Jesus.

His friend's name was Bar-thol-o-mew.

That is a long name, isn't it?

The last part of it sounds like the way the kitty says, **Mew.**

Bar-thol-o-mew was a good man.

Jesus asked him to follow Him.

He was glad to follow Jesus because he loved Him.

The Wedding

About that time Jesus went home to Nazareth.

His five new friends went with Him.

Jesus had been away from home for some time.

He wanted to see His Mother.

He wanted to have His five new Apostles know her.

When He got home His Mother was not there.

Someone told Him that she had gone to a wedding in Cana.

They asked Him to come to the wedding, too.

His five Apostles went with Him.

Everybody was happy.

Everybody was having a good time.

They were laughing and singing.

By and by the wine gave out.

The bride and groom were sorry.

They did not know what to do.

Someone told Mary about it.

Mary went to Jesus.

She said to Him, **Son, they have no more wine.**

Then she told the servants to do as Jesus told them.

He told them to fill six water jugs with water.

Then He told them to carry the jugs to the head
waiter.

When the water was poured it was changed into
wine.

That was a great wonder.

Only God can do great wonders.

That was the first great wonder that Jesus did.

He did it to please His Blessed Mother.

There are many lessons in that story of Cana.

One of them is a lesson in love.

It is the love of Jesus for His sweet Mother.

He knew there was no wine.

He did nothing about it.

He waited until Mary asked Him to do something.

The bride was a friend of Mary.

Jesus did that great wonder to please Mary and to make her friend happy.

Jesus is the same now as He was then.

He still does great wonders to please Mary.

He likes to make her friends happy.

All the Saints have loved Mary.

We know that Jesus loves best those that love His Mother most.

Jesus loves His Mother very, very much.

Jesus is God. Jesus is Man, too.

All men love their mothers.

All men love to see their mothers loved by others.

We worship Jesus.

We dearly love His mother.

The more we love her the more we are like Jesus.

He loves her with all His Heart.

After the great wonder at Cana, Jesus and Mary went to live at Caph-ar-naum. (Kaf-ar-num)

It was a lovely city. It was by a lake.

Jesus' work had just begun.

84

He had come into the world to atone for the sins
of the world.

To "atone" means to make up for.

Suppose you threw a stone and broke a window.

The people in the house with the broken window
would be angry.

Your father would have to send money to them.

The money would pay for the window.

It would "atone" for your deed.

Now Adam and Eve broke God's law.

They disobeyed God. God was angry.

He drove Adam and Eve from the garden.

He closed the gates of Heaven.

No one could go to Heaven until the sin of Adam
and Eve was atoned for.

That is why God sent His Son, Jesus, into the world.

Jesus came to pay God for the sins of Adam and
Eve and all the world.

Jesus did not pay with money.

Jesus paid with sorrow and pain.

We must remember that.

When we have sorrow or pain, then we are most
like Jesus.

We must offer it up to God for souls.
Then we are little apostles.
God is pleased and He blesses us.
Then we will be happy.

Jesus Came to Show Us the Way

Jesus came into the world to atone for sin.
Jesus came to teach the good, glad news of God's
    love for us.
He came to show us the way to Heaven. He taught
    for three years.
His twelve Apostles followed Him everywhere.
They saw all the sweet things He did.
They heard all the kind things He said.
As they listened to Him their faith grew stronger.
Jesus did not write anything down.
Faith comes by hearing, St. Paul, one of His
    greatest teachers, said.
Jesus wanted His Apostles to see His great wonders.
He wanted them to hear all His stories.
He wanted them to be sure that He is God.
He wanted them to tell the world about Heaven.
Soon He would go back to His Father in Heaven.
Then they would go about as He had done.

86

One day Jesus said to them, **Go and teach all people.**

He said, **I am with you all days.**

I am with you till the end of the world.

We believe that Jesus has kept His promise.

The Church that Jesus left on earth is still teaching.

Its priests are still following Jesus.

We listen to them because Jesus told us to.

He that hears you, hears Me. He that hates you, hates Me, He said.

The Church is our guide. The Church is like a kind mother.

The Church was started by Jesus. That is why we call it Holy.

Jesus Came to Teach

Jesus was a strict teacher.

He wanted to have things done right.

One day he went to the big church in Jerusalem.

It was a big feast day in the church.

It was called the "Pasch." Many people were there.

Some of them had not come to worship God.

They had come to sell things. Jesus did not like that.

A church is a holy place. It is God's house.

It is a house of prayer. Jesus was angry.

He wanted to teach these people a lesson.

He took a whip and drove them out of the church.

He upset the tables where the money was.

He told the people to take their things away.

He did not want them to treat the holy church
   as if it were a shop.

Jesus said to them, **My house is a house of prayer.**

You must come to church to worship.

You see, children, Jesus was angry because
   people were forgetting God, His Father.

He knew that they were thinking more of money
   than of God.

Some people are like that even today. It is very sad.

The Sermon on the Mountain

One day Jesus and His twelve Apostles went for
   a walk.

A great many people followed them.

They went up to the top of a hill.

Jesus sat down to rest. All the people sat down, too.

They just loved to be near Him. Most of the people
　　were poor.

Many of them were sad. Jesus spoke to them
　　sweetly.

His words gave them hope.

They knew that He loved them.

They knew that Jesus was their friend.

They knew that He was God. They knew that He
　　spoke the truth.

Blessed are you poor, He said.

Blessed are the meek.

Blessed are the sad.

Blessed are those who long for goodness.

Blessed are the kind.

Blessed are the clean of heart.

Blessed are those who make peace.

Blessed are they who suffer for God.

These are the eight "Blesseds." Some day you must
learn them.

Jesus Came to Teach Us to Pray

Jesus talked to the people in little words.

They were like little children.

They liked to listen to His stories.

They liked best His stories about Heaven.

Jesus told them about His Father in Heaven.

Jesus said to them, **The Father and I are one.**

They thought that was very strange.

They did not see how that could be.

They didn't mind, though.

They loved Jesus.

90

They knew that Jesus loved them.

They knew that they wanted to go to Heaven some day.

Our minds are so little, they said.

We cannot understand those things now.

If we could, we should not need faith.

Jesus wants us to believe that He and the Father are one.

Some day, when we see Him in Heaven, we shall understand.

Jesus taught the people a beautiful prayer.

It has been handed down to us.

Because Jesus taught it we must love it.

It is called the Lord's prayer.

You must learn it and say it often.

Our Father who art in Heaven, hallowed be Thy name.

Thy kingdom come.

Thy will be done on earth as it is in Heaven.

Give us this day our daily bread

And forgive us our trespasses,

As we forgive those who trespass against us;

And lead us not into temptation,

But deliver us from evil. Amen.

The Poor Widow's Son

Jesus was always helping people.
One day He and His Apostles were going to Naim.
Just outside the city they met a long line of people.
A young man was dead. He was his mother's only son.
Her husband had died long before. Now her dear son was dead.

92

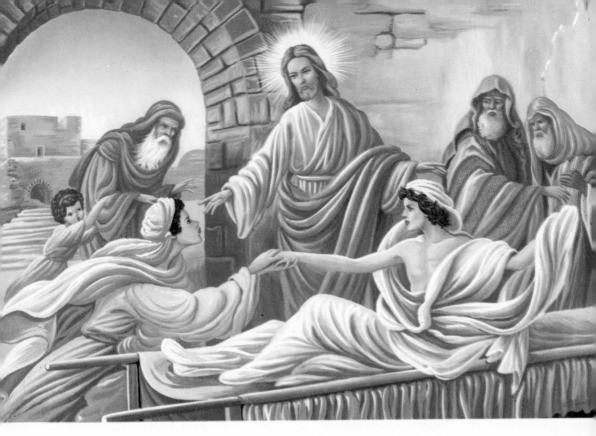

Jesus looked at her. She was crying. He felt so sorry
 for her.
He walked over and touched the boy. Everyone
 stood still.
Jesus spoke to the boy who was dead.
Young man, I say to you, arise, He said.
The boy sat up and looked around. Jesus gave him
 back to his mother.
That was a great wonder.
I think they must have been very good after that,
 don't you?

I think their hearts were always saying:

**Thank You, sweet Jesus, thank You. You are so kind
and good.**

**You are Jesus, the Promised One. You are the Son
of God the Father.**

The Storm

Great crowds followed Jesus everywhere.

He taught from morning till night. One evening He
was very tired.

Let us go into our boat, He said.

Let us go over to the other side of the sea.

The Apostles were glad to do as He wished.

They all got into the boat.

Jesus fell asleep.

Soon a great storm arose. The sky was as black as ink.

The wind blew and blew.

The waves were higher than the boat.

The Apostles were afraid.

They thought it strange that Jesus kept sleeping.

Finally they could stand it no longer.

They called to Him,

Jesus, help us or we shall die!

Jesus stood up in the boat. He raised His hand.

He said to the waves, **Peace, be still!**
Then the sea was quiet. The storm was over.
Then Jesus spoke to His Apostles.
He said, **Why are you afraid?**
Don't you know that I am God?
When you are with Me you need not fear.
You must have faith, He said.
The Apostles looked at one another.
Surely, Jesus is God, they said.
Even the sea and winds obey Him.
He is truly the Promised One.

The Rich Man's Little Girl

Not long after that, Jesus was again in Capharnaum
  (Kaf-ar-num).
There was a rich man there named Jairus (Jarus).
His little girl was very sick.
Her father was afraid that she was going to die.
He was worried and sad.
Then he thought about Jesus.
If only Jesus would come, he said.
I am sure that He would cure her.
Jairus left home to find Jesus.
He fell at Jesus' feet and cried:

Jesus, my child is sick, please come
and make her well.
Jesus felt sorry for the man.
He answered his prayer.
He went to the house of Jairus.
The little girl was dead. Her mother was crying.
Then Jesus did a wonderful thing.
He went to the little girl's bed.
He took her by the hand. **Arise**, He said sweetly.
The little girl opened her eyes.

Jesus gave her back to her parents.

They had faith in His goodness and power and He rewarded them.

Jesus is glad to find people with faith.

He still answers their prayers.

Faith will move mountains, He once said.

Ask and you shall receive.

Loaves and Fishes

One day when the Apostles were with Jesus He went for a long walk.

He went into the desert. Jesus loved the desert because it was quiet.

A great many people followed Jesus and the Apostles.

Jesus was glad to see so many people.

He talked to them about Heaven. He healed the sick people.

When evening came, the Apostles went to Jesus.

They said, **We must send the people home. They are hungry.**

We have no food for them.

97

Jesus said, **How much food is there?**

The Apostles said, **Five loaves and two fishes.**

Then Jesus told all the people to sit down.

He blessed the food and told the Apostles to give
it to the people.

There were about five thousand people there.

There was plenty of food for all.

When they had eaten all they wanted there was
enough left to fill two baskets.

That was a great wonder (miracle).

The Promise of the Blessed Sacrament

The people thought it wonderful of Jesus to feed
them when they were hungry.

They loved Him for it and wanted to make Him
king.

Jesus did not want to be king, so He went and hid
so that they could not find Him.

He and His Apostles went back to Capharnaum
(Kaf-ar-num).

The next day He went to the church to teach.

Great crowds came to hear Him.

They had come because of the great wonder He had done the day before.

He had blessed five loaves of bread and fed five thousand people.

They told their friends about it and they were so happy that they came, too.

Jesus is God—He knows all things.

He could read their hearts.

He knew why they had come.

He knew they thought a great deal about food and such things.

He knew they thought too much about what they would eat.

He said to them, **Don't be thinking always about bread that will mold and rot.**

Lift Up Your Hearts

You must lift up your minds and hearts.

You must not be thinking only of what to eat and what to wear.

Those things are good but they pass away.

You must think of things that will never pass away.

Jesus said to them, **I am the bread of life.**

He said, **Someday I will give you My flesh to eat.**

I will give you My Blood to drink.

I will give It to you so that you may have life in you.

Some of the people were angry when they heard
Him say that.

How can He do that? they said.

We don't believe in such talk.

Then they went away.

Jesus was sorry to see His friends go away.

But He did not call them back. No.

He knew that they understood His words.

He knew that they were the kind of people that
would not lift up their hearts.

They were like spoiled children.

Jesus was sorry to see them go.

He said to His friends as the angry people were
going away,

**Yes, it is true. My flesh is meat indeed and My
Blood is drink indeed.**

**He who eats My flesh and drinks My Blood will live
in Me and I will live in him.**

Jesus was talking about Holy Communion.

100

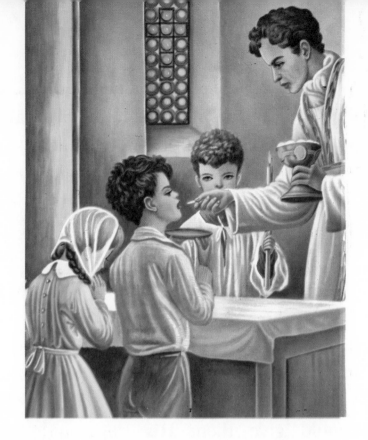

Holy Communion means that Jesus gives Himself
    to us in the Blessed Sacrament.

It means that we give ourselves to Him.

Let us think about it often.

Let us ask Mary to help us get ready for Jesus in
    Holy Communion.

St. Peter's Answer

Jesus watched the angry people going away.

Many of them were old friends of His.

They had seen Him heal the sick people.

101

They had seen Him make the blind man see.
They had seen Him make the lame people walk.
They had been with Jesus for a long time.
Now they had gone away. Jesus was sad.
He turned to the Apostles. Tears were in His eyes.
Will you also go away? He said.
It was their leader who answered Jesus.
It was St. Peter who said, **Lord, where shall we go?**
You are Christ, the Son of God.
You have the words of eternal life.
Jesus was glad when Peter said that.
He knew that Peter did not understand how
He could give them His flesh and Blood
to eat any more than the others did.
Jesus knew that Peter had faith and believed that
He could do all things.
Jesus was pleased with Peter's faith.
We must be like Peter.
We must have faith in God.
We must believe all that God has taught.
Then God will be pleased with us, too.
He will give us many graces.
Most of all He will teach us how to love Him.

I Will Build My Church

One day Jesus was in a strange city.

He wished to test the faith of the Apostles.

He said to them, **Who do these people say that I am?**

The Apostles said, **Oh, they say different things.**

Some say You are Moses.

Some say You are Elias.

Some say that You are a prophet.

But who do you say that I am? Jesus said.

Peter answered for them all.

Peter said, **You are Christ, the Son of God.**

Jesus was pleased with Peter's answer.

He said, **Blessed are you, Simon.**

You are Peter, and upon this rock I will build My Church.

It will never be destroyed.

Even the devils in Hell cannot destroy it.

I am with you all days.

I am with you till the end of the world.

Jesus has kept His promise.

His Church is still teaching about God and Heaven.

The Church Jesus started is the Holy Catholic
Church.

It is called "Catholic" because it is everywhere in
the world.

It is for all people.

It is called "Holy" because Jesus, its Founder, is holy.

The Last Supper

Jesus came down to earth to teach us the way to live.

He came also to atone for our sins.

The work of teaching was done.

104

The day of Jesus' suffering for our sins had come.
Jesus told His Apostles to get supper ready.
In the evening Jesus came to eat with them.
It was the Last Supper.
Jesus took bread in His hands.
He blessed and broke It.
He gave It to His Apostles.
He said, **Take ye and eat.**
This is my Body.
Then He blessed some wine.

He gave it to His Apostles.

Drink ye all of This, He said.

This is My Blood.

Jesus had kept His promise.

He had told them He would give them His Body
   to eat and His Blood to drink.

Now it was so.

He gave the Apostles their First Holy Communion.

That is why the priest says Mass every day.

Do this in memory of Me, He said.

In the Mass the priests do what Jesus
   told them to do.

They change bread and wine into Jesus' Body and
   Blood.

They do it in memory of Jesus.

The Blessed Sacrament

Many people receive Holy Communion every day.

Jesus loves to live in our hearts.

Jesus lives in our churches always.

The little red lamp that burns on our altars tells us
   that Jesus is there.

Jesus in the Blessed Sacrament lives in the little
   tabernacle.

When we go into church we always kneel on our
    right knee before going into the pew.

In that way we adore Jesus as the Angels adore Him
    in Heaven.

When we kneel to adore Him, let us say with all our
    hearts:

Jesus, I adore You.

We must love Jesus in the Blessed Sacrament.

We must visit Him often.

Then we shall make Jesus happy.

He will know that we love Him.

He will give us His gifts.

He will make us strong in faith.

He will make us happy and good.

The Agony in the Garden

When the Last Supper was over Jesus left His
friends, the Apostles.

He went to the Garden of Olives.

Soon the bad men would come.

They would drag Him away.

Jesus was very sad. He prayed to His Father in
Heaven.

Then He bowed His head.

Thy will be done, He said.

Father, I am ready to suffer and die.

I want everyone to be happy and go to Heaven.

Then the bad men came.

They dragged Him into the city.

108

They treated Him as if He were a bad man, too.

Jesus was so good and kind. But those bad men
    hated Him.

They tied Him to a post. They whipped Him.

They put a crown of thorns on His Head.

They made fun of Him.

Jesus was meek and humble. Jesus suffered because
    He loves us.

He suffered in silence.

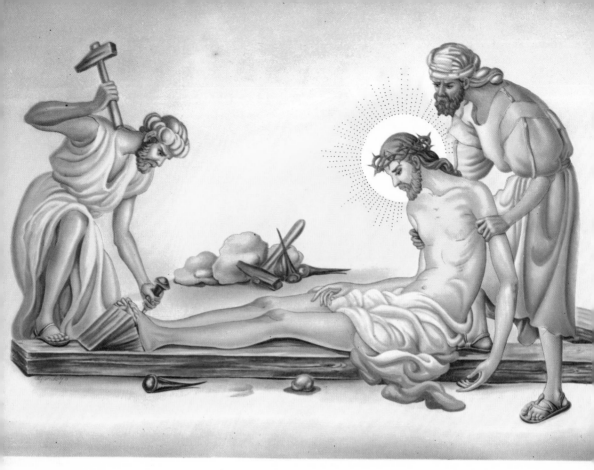

Jesus' Death

At last the cruel men said that Jesus must die.

They placed a cross on His shoulders.

They made Him carry it to the top of a hill.

Then they nailed Him to it. Poor Jesus died on the
cross on Friday.

We call it Good Friday because Jesus was so good
to die for us.

His sweet mother watched Him die. How sad she
must have been!

110

Some friends of Jesus took Him down from the
   cross.
They laid Him in His mother's arms.
Poor Mary! Her Son was dead. His body was cov-
   ered with blood.
She was very, very sad.
The sword of sorrow had pierced her heart.
She knew that He is the Son of God.
Those whom He loved and served had killed Him.

The Burial

Sadly, Mary walked beside the men who carried Him away.

They laid Him in a new grave that belonged to a friend of Jesus.

When Jesus was laid in the tomb His mother and friends went to their homes.

Mary knew that Jesus is God.

She knew that He could do all things.

She knew that He would rise from the dead.

The bad men that killed Jesus were afraid that friends of Jesus would steal His body away.

They thought that His friends would try to fool the world.

So they did a very silly thing.

They placed a big stone in front of the tomb.

They sent soldiers to guard the door.

All night long the guards stood and watched.

It was still and dark there.

Everybody was restless and sad.

There had been an earthquake.

It was very dark because Jesus had been killed.

The world was sad because Jesus was in the tomb.

112

The First Easter

It was early on Sunday morning.

Mary Magdalen and two other women went to the tomb.

Mary Magdalen loved Jesus very much because He forgave her sins.

The women carried sweet spices and oils.

They were going to pour them on the body of Jesus.

Mary Magdalen remembered the stone before the tomb.

She knew how heavy it was.

As they hurried along the road she said,

Who will roll back the stone?

Soon they reached the tomb.

They saw that the stone had been rolled away. The door was open.

Mary Magdalen ran back to the city.

She told the Apostles, **They have taken away my Lord and we do not know where they have laid Him.**

The other two women went nearer to the door of the tomb.

113

There—where Jesus had been—they saw a beautiful
   Angel.

They were afraid.

The Angel said, **Do not be afraid; you are looking
   for Jesus.**

He is risen. He is not here.

**Go tell Peter and the rest of the Apostles that
   He is risen and gone to Galilee.
   You will see Him there.**

114

It was early in the morning when Jesus rose from the dead.

We can be sure that He went first to see His sweet mother.

Mary Magdalen saw Him, too.

She loved Him very dearly because He was so kind.

Before she knew Jesus she was very bad.

He forgave her all her sins and then she was good.

Because she was so true to Him and believed in His goodness, He rewarded her on Easter morning.

He let her see Him and He spoke to her.

On Easter the Apostles were gathered together in one room.

All the doors were closed. The Apostles were afraid.

They were very quiet there.

All of a sudden Jesus stood among them.

He said, **Peace be to you!**

The Apostles did not know what to think.

They thought He was a ghost.

He said to them, **A ghost does not eat; give Me some food.**

He ate food to show them that He was alive.

They crowded around Him because they were so happy to have Him with them again.

He breathed on them and said, **Peace be to you!**

Whose sins you shall forgive, they are forgiven.

Whose sins you shall not forgive, they are not forgiven.

That is why we know that priests have the power to forgive sins.

Jesus gave them that power on the day that He rose from the dead.

116

When Jesus went to see the Apostles, Thomas was not there.

He would not believe that they had seen Him.

He said that he would have to see Jesus himself.

He said that he would have to see the prints of the nails in the hands and feet of Jesus.

Thomas would not believe that Jesus had risen from the dead.

Eight days later Jesus came again to the room where the Apostles were.

Come here! He said to Thomas. **See My hands and My feet.**

Put your hand in My side.

Then Thomas was ashamed that he had not believed that Jesus had risen.

Thomas knelt at the feet of Jesus.

He said, **My Lord and my God!**

Jesus said to him, **You believe now because you see.**

More blessed are they who believe and do not see.

Jesus wants us to have faith.

Jesus did not write anything down.

Jesus told His first priests to go and teach all nations.

117

He said, **Teach them all the things I have taught you.**

Those that believe shall be saved.

Those that do not believe shall not be saved.

He said, **I am with you all days, even to the end of the world.**

The Church has always taught what Jesus taught.

The priests are the same as the Apostles.

They have heard the Master's call, **Follow Me!**

They have heard the Master's words, **Teach all nations.**

They love to tell us about Jesus.

Jesus Goes Back to Heaven

Forty days after Easter, Jesus led the Apostles out to the Mount of Olives.

They asked Him many questions.

He told them that He would send the Holy Spirit to them soon.

The Holy Spirit would make them strong and happy, He said.

After they received the Holy Spirit, they must tell the people all over the world about what they had seen and heard

They must not go out and preach until He sent
    Holy Spirit.
They must teach the people the way to Heaven.
Then He blessed them and was lifted up.
A cloud carried Him up to Heaven.
The Apostles stood there for a long time.
They watched the cloud as long as they could see it.
When they looked about they saw two Angels.
The Angels said, **Why do you stand there looking
    up to Heaven?**

119

This Jesus Who is taken away will come as you see
   Him going.
He will come upon the clouds of Heaven.
He will come upon the last day.
Then the Angels went away.
The Apostles went sadly down the hill.
Jesus, their Leader, had gone back to Heaven.
Peter was their leader now.
They were afraid to go about the streets.
They went to their little room where they had often
   been with Jesus.
Jesus had told them to wait there and pray.
They did as Jesus told them.

The Holy Spirit

The Apostles waited in the little room and prayed.
They prayed until the Holy Spirit came.
The Blessed Mother of Jesus was with them.
One day when they were praying they heard a
   noise.
It was like a big wind.

120

Parted tongues of fire rested above their heads.
They were filled with the Holy Spirit.
They were not afraid any longer.
They were now ready to go out and preach.
Jesus had gone back to Heaven.
But they knew that He was with them, too.
I am with you all days, He had said.
I am with you until the end of the world.
They felt strong and brave.

121

They did not care how people talked to them now.
They did not care what people did to them.
They had work to do for God.
They went out of that room with joy and love
   of God.
The Holy Spirit taught them what to say.
The Holy Spirit gave them many gifts.
The Holy Spirit filled them with peace and joy.
They were happy to do God's work.

The Apostles Begin to Teach

St. Peter and the other Apostles went out to preach.
Some of them went to far away places.
They taught new apostles and blessed them.
Then the new ones taught others and blessed them.
That is how the teaching of Jesus has come down
      to us.
Jesus said there should be one fold and one
   shepherd.
The Holy Catholic Church is the fold.
The Pope is the shepherd.
He is in St. Peter's place at the head of the Church.

122

St. Peter was made head of the Church by Jesus
    Himself.
The apostles are still teaching.
They want the other sheep to come into the fold.
They want the wish of Jesus to come true.
His wish is, **I pray that they may be one.**
Jesus wants all people to come to Him.
Some people think that they are not good enough
    to belong to His Church.
No one should think like that.
No one should be afraid of Jesus.
We go to church not because we are good.
We go because Jesus is good.
He loves us and wants us to be with Him.

Jesus' Church Is in France

Many of the Saints have lived in France.
Saints are people who love Jesus very much.
They do everything just for Jesus.
St. Therese lived in France.
We call her "The Little Flower."
She loves little people.
We must ask her to pray for us.
She will help us to be good.

Jesus' Church Is in Italy

St. Peter himself preached in Rome.
St. Peter died in Rome.
Cruel men killed him.
He died for love of Jesus.
The Pope is the Bishop of Rome.
We call him "The Holy Father."
We must pray for him.
We must pray for the missions.
They are very dear to his heart.

Jesus' Church Is in Africa

There are many missions
    in Africa.
There are many priests
    and sisters there.

They are teaching people about Jesus.
Jesus helps them to be strong and happy.
They are not sad though they are far away from
    home.

124

God is everywhere.

Priests and sisters live and work for God.

They love to work for God.

They have their little chapels
    in the missions.

Jesus in the Blessed Sacrament
    lives on their altars.

He comes to them every day in Holy Communion.

He feeds their souls and makes them strong.

They are always happy.

They serve the Lord with gladness.

It is wonderful to be a priest or a sister.

It is wonderful to live and work "all for Jesus."

Jesus' Church Is in Japan

Japan is a very beautiful country.

Many priests and sisters are in Japan.

They are teaching people about the one true God.

They are glad to tell the people about Jesus.

People are happy when they belong to the Holy
    Catholic Church.

They are happy because they love to worship Jesus.

They know that Jesus loves them.

Jesus' Church Is in China

There are many, many people in China.

The Chinese people need missionary priests,
brothers and sisters to preach to them that Jesus
came to save us all, because He loves us all.

Jesus' Church Is in South America

Hundreds of years ago priests went to South America.

The priests taught the people about Jesus.

The priests built schools for them.

The priests taught them many things.

South America has many beautiful cities now.

Most of the people belong to the Holy Catholic
Church.

St. Rose lived in South America.

She was a holy nun.

She wore a snow-white habit.

She belonged to the order of St. Dominic.

Let us pray to St. Rose of Lima.

Let us ask her to pray for the missions.

Jesus' Church Is in North America

Columbus found our country in 1492.

He was a Catholic.

Priests came soon after that.

They called the people they found there Indians.

The Indians lived in the woods.

They dressed in animal skins.

The priests were kind to them.

They taught them about Jesus.

Jesus blessed the priests who were so brave and
good.

Many of the Indians are good, holy Catholics.

One American Indian girl led a saintly life.

Her name was Tekakwitha.

She was pure and holy.

She loved Jesus very much.

There are millions of Catholics in North America now.

The Catholic Church

You see, children, that the Catholic Church is everywhere.

The Catholic Church is the same everywhere.

It teaches people to love one another.

It teaches people to be kind and helpful.
It teaches people to be clean of heart.
It teaches them to obey the will of God.
It teaches them in many ways.
Its artists paint pictures of Jesus doing good deeds.
They paint pictures of Mary and of the saints.
Beautiful music tells the story of the life of Jesus.
Long ago when people could not read the Bible
    they knew of Jesus in pictures and music.

The Bible

There are many more stories about Jesus.
There are too many for me to tell you now.
They are very beautiful and sweet.

You will find them in the Holy Bible.

When you are old enough to read well, you must be sure to read the Bible.

The Church gathered together all the books of the Bible.

Holy monks and nuns carefully copied them on paper made from skins of sheep.

There were not many Bibles in the days of the early Church.

It took such a long time to copy them by hand.

Printing had not been invented.

Now we may have Bibles in every Catholic home.

All of us should read the Bible every day.

We should listen very carefully to the priests when they preach to us on Sunday.

We should read the prayers in our prayerbooks, too.

Many of them are copied from the Bible.

All of them are beautiful.

They will help us to be good.

Jesus' House

Once Jesus said, **My house is a house of prayer.**

I want to tell you a little about the house of Jesus.

Jesus' house is called a church.

130

The church always has an altar.
In the center of the altar there is always a little room
   with a door.
It is the tabernacle.
Jesus, in the Blessed Sacrament, is in the tabernacle.
A red lamp glows near the altar.
It burns all day and all night because Jesus is there.
Let us say this prayer kneeling before the taber-
   nacle:

O Sacrament most holy, O Sacrament divine,

**All praise and all thanksgiving be every moment
   Thine!**

Pictures in the Church

In our homes we have pictures of those we love.
Mothers like to look at pictures of their children.
Children like to look at pictures of mother and
   daddy.
We all like to look at pictures of friends.
When we look at pictures of friends we think of
   them.
We like to think that they are thinking of us.
The Saints are friends of Jesus.
We put pictures of them in His house.

Jesus wants us to know them and to love them.

That is why we like to look at pictures of the Saints.

We think of them and how they loved and served
   God.

We ask them to help us to be good.

We pray to the Saints.

We do not worship them. We worship only God.

Our Mother

God has given us a mother to guide us.

It is our Holy Mother Church.

The Church tells us that we must know God.

It tells us that we must love God.

It tells us that we must serve God in this world.

Then we shall be happy with Him forever in
   Heaven.

We must always pray and work to save our souls.

We must carry on the work of the holy Apostles.

That is why I have told you these little stories about
   God.

Now you must tell them to the other little people.

Then you will be a little apostle.

Daughters of St. Paul

IN MASSACHUSETTS
50 St. Paul's Ave., Jamaica Plain, Boston, MA 02130;
617-522-8911; 617-522-0875.
172 Tremont Street, Boston, MA 02111; **617-426-5464;
617-426-4230.**

IN NEW YORK
78 Fort Place, Staten Island, NY 10301; **212-447-5071; 212-447-5086.**
59 East 43rd Street, New York, NY 10017; **212-986-7580.**
625 East 187th Street, Bronx, NY 10458; **212-584-0440.**
525 Main Street, Buffalo, NY 14203; **716-847-6044.**

IN NEW JERSEY
Hudson Mall — Route 440 and Communipaw Ave.,
Jersey City, NJ 07304; **201-433-7740.**

IN CONNECTICUT
202 Fairfield Ave., Bridgeport, CT 06604; **203-335-9913.**

IN OHIO
2105 Ontario Street (at Prospect Ave.), Cleveland, OH 44115;
216-621-9427.
25 E. Eighth Street, Cincinnati, OH 45202; **513-721-4838;
513-421-5733.**

IN PENNSYLVANIA
1719 Chestnut Street, Philadelphia, PA 19103; **215-568-2638.**

IN VIRGINIA
1025 King Street, Alexandria, VA 22314; **703-683-1741;
703-549-3806.**

IN FLORIDA
2700 Biscayne Blvd., Miami, FL 33137; **305-573-1618.**

IN LOUISIANA
4403 Veterans Memorial Blvd., Metairie, LA 70002; **504-887-7631;
504-887-0113.**
1800 South Acadian Thruway, P.O. Box 2028, Baton Rouge, LA 70821;
504-343-4057; 504-381-9485.

IN MISSOURI
1001 Pine Street (at North 10th), St. Louis, MO 63101; **314-621-0346;
314-231-1034.**

IN ILLINOIS
172 North Michigan Ave., Chicago, IL 60601; **312-346-4228;
312-346-3240.**

IN TEXAS
114 Main Plaza, San Antonio, TX 78205; **512-224-8101.**

IN CALIFORNIA
1570 Fifth Ave., San Diego, CA 92101; **619-232-1442.**
46 Geary Street, San Francisco, CA 94108; **415-781-5180.**

IN HAWAII
1143 Bishop Street, Honolulu, HI 96813; **808-521-2731.**

IN ALASKA
750 West 5th Ave., Anchorage, AK 99501; **907-272-8183.**

IN CANADA
3022 Dufferin Street, Toronto 395, Ontario, Canada.

IN ENGLAND
128, Notting Hill Gate, London W11 3QG, England.
133 Corporation Street, Birmingham B4 6PH, England.
5A-7 Royal Exchange Square, Glasgow G1 3AH, England.
82 Bold Street, Liverpool L1 4HR, England.

IN AUSTRALIA
58 Abbotsford Rd., Homebush, N.S.W. 2140, Australia